mezze

mezze

a culinary journey of discovery

BEVERLY LE BLANC

Love Food ™ is an imprint of Parragon Books Ltd

Parragon
Queen Street House
4 Queen Street
Bath BA1 1HE, UK

ISBN: 978-1-4054-9250-8
Printed in China

Produced by the Bridgewater Book Company Ltd

Photography: Clive Bozzard-Hill

Home economists: Valerie Barrett and Rosie Hopper

Notes for the Reader
This book uses imperial, metric, and US cup measurements. Follow the same units of measurement throughout; do not mix imperial and metric. All spoon measurements are level: teaspoons are assumed to be 5 ml, and tablespoons are assumed to be 15 ml. Unless otherwise stated, milk is assumed to be whole, eggs and individual vegetables such as potatoes are medium, and pepper is freshly ground black pepper. Recipes using raw or very lightly cooked eggs should be avoided by infants, the elderly, pregnant women, convalescents, and anyone suffering from an illness. The times given are an approximate guide only.

Picture Acknowledgments
The publisher would like to thank the following for permission to reproduce copyright material: Peter Adams/zefa/Corbis (pages 6–7), Royalty-Free/Corbis (pages 18 and 32), Roy Morsch/zefa/Corbis (page 39), Corbis (page 80), P.Hussenot/ photocuisine/Corbis (page 81), and Envision/Corbis (page 82).

Contents

Introduction

Preparing and eating mezze is a culinary treat that embraces the cooking styles and vibrant flavors of North Africa, the eastern Mediterranean, and the Middle East. The most basic definition of mezze is simply a selection of meat, poultry, seafood, and vegetable appetizers and street food. But that description doesn't give any hint of the exciting flavors awaiting you when you sample the recipes in this book.

Just imagine sitting at a picturesque, palm-shaded table laden with small dishes containing rich, creamy dips, pepper halves mounded high with spiced meat and rice, chickpeas adorned with glistening pomegranate seeds, just-barbecued morsels of marinated lamb, thin wedges of a spinach omelet, and crisp, lightly coated squid rings hot from the skillet. This simple feast sums up the essence of mezze culture that is a part of everyday life throughout the Mediterranean region.

Mezze culture

Mezze recipes, especially those from Turkey, provide a culinary bridge across the East—West divide. Like Spanish tapas, French hors d'oeuvres, and Italian antipasti, mezze are part of the relaxed eating style of the countries along the Mediterranean and Aegean seas. Traditional mezze dishes from Greece, Lebanon, and Turkey—chickpea dip, eggplant dip, falafel, and fried squid rings, to name a few—are universally popular, but Algerian, Cypriot, Egyptian, Israeli, Libyan, Moroccan, Tunisian, and Syrian cooks are also masters of somewhat

lesser-known, tempting mezze preparations. One common link between these diverse cultures is an enjoyment of outdoor eating, reflected in the numerous barbecued recipes on all mezze menus. Tender, aromatic kabobs, spicy meatballs on skewers, fresh seafood, and vegetables all arrive at the mezze table with an appealing charbroiled flavor. You'll find recipes in this book that will help you capture in your own kitchen some of the authentic barbecued mezze flavors by using a searing-hot, heavy grill pan.

And yet "mezze" means different things to different people. It can range from a simple snack to a whole feast consisting of many small dishes for sharing. Throughout the region, every café, street food stall, and restaurant offers a selection of mezze dishes, and in the home, dishes are prepared using recipes passed down through the generations with little variation of ingredients and flavorings.

In Western cultures, mezze are commonly thought of as small portions of appetizers or tasty nibbles intended to stimulate the appetite before sitting down to the main meal. Simple mezze dishes, perhaps no more than a bowl of olives or home-made chickpea dip with pieces of warmed pita bread, are also served as finger food to accompany alcoholic drinks. Greeks, for example, are particularly fond of eating plump, juicy olives while sipping a glass of ouzo, the popular unsweetened, anise-flavored liquor. Chunks of crusty, freshly baked bread and a dip was once a staple meal for peasants unable to afford meat, but in today's more affluent times this most simple of mezze is regarded as a perfect accompaniment to a chilled white wine.

In North Africa and throughout the Middle East, however, the widespread prohibition of alcohol and traditional customs of generous hospitality and of sharing food, especially with strangers, puts mezze in a different context. Preparing a varied selection of small dishes that lend themselves to

communal dining certainly helps domestic cooks overcome the frequent challenge of catering for unexpected guests who have been brought along by other diners. A lavish selection of mezze dishes is also ideal for parties and celebrations, where guests can help themselves. Also, for many in the Middle East the idea of whetting one's appetite before eating a meal is an alien concept. For religious reasons, moderation is advocated at meal times, so many people eat only when they are hungry, thus eliminating the need to stimulate their gastric juices. In regions where alcohol is banned, small cups of dark, strong coffee or glasses of iced water or chilled syrups are always served with a small, mezze-style accompaniment alongside.

Even the word "mezze" changes as you travel through the region — "meze" is one common alternative spelling, and you will find *mazza* in most Arab countries, *mezethaki* in Greece, *qimiyya* in Algeria, and *ādū* in Tunisia. But whatever word you find on menus, expect the choice to be varied, with a mixture of hot or cold dishes to choose from.

The history of mezze culture intertwines with centuries of conquering armies and trade routes between the Far East and Western Europe and North Africa. The influences of the ancient Phoenicians, Greeks, Persians, Arabs, and Ottoman Turks are all discernable. As today's popular mezze has evolved out of so many diverse culinary traditions, there is little consensus among food historians on the origins. One of the many plausible theories is that the word mezze comes from the Arabic verb *tamazzaza*, which means to taste food slowly in small quantities, giving your tastebuds heightened enjoyment. That certainly explains the pleasure of enjoying a meal of mezze dishes. Another theory about the origins of the word "mezze" is that it comes from the Italian word for middle, *mezzano*, and was passed along trade routes from Genoese spice traders to Arab merchants, where it evolved into the variant spellings in the different regions.

Planning your mezze meal

One of the joys of cooking mezze is that there aren't any rules—you can enjoy hot dishes together with chilled dishes, a mix of spicy and mild food, and meat-and seafood-based dishes alongside vegetarian dishes. Part of mezze's global popularity has to be that its flexibility provides for all tastes. It also gives cooks scope for preparing satisfying meals without spending hours in the kitchen, and many recipes can be prepared in advance to be serve chilled or at room temperature.

Restaurants in the Middle East pride themselves on the quantity and variety of their mezze tables, producing up to 50 dishes for a single meal, but there isn't any reason for the home cook to go to such extremes. If you are planning to serve mezze with drinks before a meal, you will need only three or four dishes. Always popular are olives with lemon and cheese pastries, or any of the dips found in the first chapter.

If, however, you plan a whole meal of mezze dishes, this collection of recipes provides plenty of variety. As all the portions are smaller than if you were serving them as a conventional main course, multiply the number of guests by 2.5 to determine how many recipes to prepare. And don't forget that most of the recipes can easily be increased for double or triple portions. As well as satisfying your palette, consider pleasing your eyes, too. The recipes for orange, red bell pepper, beet, mixed vegetable, and cracked wheat salads, as well as the pickled turnips, all add a welcome splash of color to the mezze table.

Visit a Middle Eastern food store and take advantage of the selection of breads available, from thick, dimpled ones, which look similar to Italian focaccia, to soft flat breads that can be used to pick up individual pieces of food. There is no longer any reason to think only of pita bread when serving mezze.

Sun-kissed flavors

Authentic-tasting mezze are easy to reproduce at home. If you have ever enjoyed mezze on vacation, these recipes should quickly transport you back to the hustle and bustle of street markets, souk restaurants, and shaded tables set up alongside the glistening blue waters of the Mediterranean. And if you haven't enjoyed such pleasures, perhaps they will inspire you to plan your next vacation.

Most of the ingredients used in mezze cooking are the familiar flavors of the Mediterranean—dried and fresh chiles, garlic, herbs, plump lemons and oranges, and their freshly squeezed juices, olive oil, beans, spices, and creamy, thick yogurt, along with the freshest, sun-kissed eggplants, zucchini, sweet bell peppers, and tomatoes. Other, sometimes less-familiar ingredients, however, impart the unique flavors of the region, and these, itemized below, are readily available in Middle Eastern food stores, gourmet food stores, and some supermarkets.

Allspice

The essential flavoring for stuffed lamb and bulgur meatballs, and used in other meat dishes. Most commonly sold ground, this is the dried red-brown berry of the evergreen allspice tree, with an aroma that resembles a mix of cinnamon, cloves, nutmeg or mace, and pepper.

Harissa paste

North Africa's hot, spicy chili paste, which finds its way into everything, from meatballs to fruit salads. For the uninitiated, it is best used with caution until you determine a level of heat that is suitable. Available in jars and tubes.

Olive oil

The liquid gold of the Mediterranean, available in endless colors from dark green to pale yellow. The only guide to quality, however, is to taste before you buy—don't be taken in by fancy packaging. Use plain olive oil for cooking and save the more expensive extra virgin oils for dressings and finishing dishes so that the flavors can be appreciated. Remember, like all fruit juice, olive oil cannot be kept indefinitely, so do not buy too much of it if you do not regularly cook with it.

Pomegranate molasses

A dark brown syrup, made from reduced pomegranate juice, that adds a sweet-sour flavor to Middle Eastern cooking, especially dishes from Lebanon and Syria. Look for it in small bottles.

Sumac

Used to impart a slightly tart, fruity flavor to grilled or broiled meat and fish, and cooking onions in Iraq, Lebanon, Syria, and Turkey. Dark, rusty red ground sumac is from the dried berries of the elm-leaf sumac. It loses its flavor and aroma in a month even when stored in an airtight container, so buy in small quantities only.

Sesame seed paste

A thick paste made from ground sesame seeds. Its flavor is bland on its own, but it provides the backbone to Sesame sauce and Chickpea dip when mixed with olive oil and lemon juice. Sesame seed paste is sold in jars and plastic tubs, and often has a deep layer of separated oil on top, which needs to be stirred in before using.

Dips and Snacks

For most people around the world, the recipes in this chapter embody the essence of mezze. These are quick and easy recipes for casual get-togethers with friends.

Here you will find the familiar dishes from your favorite mezze menu, including chickpea dip, falafel, and spinach and feta pastry triangles. These are ideal for no-fuss entertaining because they can be prepared in advance. Garlic sauce and Chickpea dip are perfect party foods for a crowd—just double or triple the recipes. Serve these with a selection of crisp vegetable sticks—carrots, celery, zucchini, bell peppers, and radishes—and a selection of breads such as pita bread or flat breads.

Chickpea dip

Hummus bi tahini

Serves 6–8 as part of a mezze

14 oz/400 g canned chickpeas, drained and rinsed

1 garlic clove, crushed to a paste with 1/4 tsp salt

3–4 tbsp sesame seed paste

2–4 tbsp freshly squeezed lemon juice

1/4 tsp ground cumin

extra virgin olive oil, for thinning (optional), plus extra to serve

salt

warmed pita bread, to serve

To garnish

paprika

chopped fresh flat-leaf parsley

It is very rare to come across a mezze table that doesn't include this universally popular creamy dip. And it is equally rare to come across two identical versions of the recipe, so feel free to add more or less garlic, sesame seed paste, or lemon juice.

Put all but 1 tablespoon of the chickpeas into a food processor. Add the garlic and process to a thick, coarse paste. Add 3 tablespoons of sesame seed paste and process again until blended. Add 2 tablespoons of lemon juice, the cumin, and salt to taste and process until creamy. Taste and add extra sesame seed paste and/or lemon juice, if desired. For a thinner dip, with the motor running, drizzle in oil or water until you reach the desired consistency.

To serve, transfer to a serving bowl, then use the back of a spoon to make an indentation in the center of the dip. Put the reserved chickpeas in the indentation and drizzle with oil. Sprinkle with paprika and chopped parsley to garnish. Serve with warmed pita bread. Alternatively, cover and refrigerate for up to 3 days. Store any leftover dip in the same way, or it can be frozen for up to 1 month.

Broiled eggplant and sesame seed dip

Baba ganoush

Serves 4–6 as part of a mezze

olive oil, for oiling, blending, covering (optional), and to serve

1 large eggplant, about 1 lb 9 oz/700 g

2¹/₂ tbsp freshly squeezed lemon juice

2¹/₂ tbsp sesame seed paste

2 garlic cloves, crushed

salt and pepper

warmed pita bread, to serve

To garnish

black olives

chopped fresh cilantro or mint

To replicate the authentic Middle Eastern flavor of eggplants cooked over charcoal, use a very hot, ridged, cast-iron grill pan to charbroil the eggplant—just be sure to open all the windows and turn the extractor fan to high before you begin.

Heat a ridged, cast-iron grill pan or heavy-bottomed skillet over high heat until a splash of water "dances" on the surface. Brush with oil and rub oil all over the eggplant. Add the eggplant and cook for 10 minutes on each side, using a pair of tongs to turn (try not to pierce the skin, although it will eventually split), until collapsed and the skin is charred. Remove from the skillet and let cool.

When the eggplant is cool enough to handle, halve and scoop the flesh out into a food processor. Process until smooth. Add the lemon juice, sesame seed paste, garlic, and salt and pepper to taste, and process until blended. With the motor running, drizzle in about 2 tablespoons of oil until the dip is creamy and well blended. If the dip is too thick, thin with a little water, added a tablespoon at a time. Taste and adjust the seasoning, if necessary.

To serve, transfer to a serving bowl, then use the back of a spoon to make an indentation in the center of the dip. Pour a little oil into the indentation, add some olives, and sprinkle with chopped cilantro to garnish. Serve with warmed pita bread. Alternatively, cover the surface with a thin layer of oil, cover the bowl, and refrigerate for up to 3 days. Stir the oil into the mixture just before serving. Store any leftover dip in the same way.

Cook's tip

If you find the charbroiled flavor of the eggplants too strong, stir in 1–2 tablespoons of strained plain yogurt. Alternatively, roast the eggplant in a preheated oven at 450°F/230°C for 30–40 minutes, or until tender and collapsing. Pierce the eggplant all over with a fork before roasting to prevent it bursting.

Sesame sauce

Salata tahini

Serves 4–6 as part of a mezze

1 large garlic clove, crushed to a paste with 1/4 tsp salt

4–6 tbsp water

4–6 tbsp freshly squeezed lemon juice

5 1/2 oz/150 g sesame seed paste

1 tbsp very finely chopped fresh flat-leaf parsley

salt

warmed pita bread, to serve

A dish of this versatile sauce is served with fried fish and broiled meat mezze throughout the Middle East. It is also a good mezze on its own, served with broiled vegetables, or it can be stirred into mixed vegetable salad, or a bowl of chickpeas.

Put the garlic in a bowl and stir in 4 tablespoons of water and 4 tablespoons of lemon juice. Use a fork to whisk in the sesame seed paste, then season to taste with salt. Taste and add extra sesame seed paste and lemon juice, as you wish, until the sauce has a smooth, pouring consistency. Stir in the parsley. Transfer to a serving bowl.

Serve with warmed pita bread, or cover and chill in the refrigerator until required.

Cook's tip

The sauce is very thin and runny when first made, but thickens while it chills. If it is too thick when you go to use it, thin with a little water or lemon juice.

Yogurt and cucumber dip

Tzatziki (Greek), Cacik (Turkish)

Serves 4–6 as part of a mezze

1 garlic clove, crushed to a paste with ½ tsp salt, or as much garlic as you like

1¼ cups strained plain yogurt

2 tbsp extra virgin olive oil

2 tbsp dried mint

1–2 tbsp freshly squeezed lemon juice, or to taste

1 small thin-skinned cucumber, about 7 oz/200 g

salt and white pepper

cayenne pepper, to garnish (optional)

warmed pita bread, to serve

Chefs and home cooks throughout the eastern Mediterranean, the Middle East, and all the way across the Indian subcontinent never tire of preparing this refreshing dip, which also doubles as a salad in many countries.

Put the garlic in a nonreactive bowl and stir in the yogurt, oil, mint, 1 tablespoon of lemon juice, and salt and white pepper to taste. Cover and let infuse at room temperature while you prepare the cucumber.

Coarsely grate the cucumber into a strainer resting in the sink and use your hands to squeeze out all the excess moisture. Stir the cucumber into the yogurt mixture, then taste and add extra lemon juice and salt and pepper, as you wish. Cover and chill in the refrigerator for at least 2 hours.

To serve, spoon the dip into a serving bowl and lightly sprinkle with cayenne pepper to garnish, if you like. Serve with warmed pita bread.

Cook's tip

If you are planning to serve this straightaway, there isn't any need to grate the cucumber and squeeze out the moisture—just finely dice the cucumber and stir it into the yogurt mixture—but if chilled, the dip will become too watery. Greek and Turkish cooks prefer to use dried mint because fresh mint turns an unappetizing dark color when it is left to stand in this dip.

Garlic sauce

Skordaliá

Serves 4–6 as part of a mezze

2 large, starchy potatoes, about
9 oz/250 g each, scrubbed

4–5 garlic cloves, crushed to a paste
with 1 tsp salt

about 2 tbsp freshly squeezed
lemon juice or white wine vinegar

about 1/2 tsp salt

about 3/4 cup extra virgin olive oil

white pepper

To serve

2 carrots, peeled and sliced

1 large zucchini, halved lengthwise
and sliced

1 red bell pepper, seeded
and sliced

1 green bell pepper, seeded
and sliced

warmed pita bread (optional)

Many recipes for this pungent sauce are made with ground almonds or walnuts, but this recipe, using boiled starchy potatoes, has a slightly milder flavor. This sauce goes well with beet salad or broiled sardines and it can also be served as a dip.

Put the potatoes in a pan, pour over enough boiling water to cover, and return to a boil. Cook for 12–15 minutes, or until the potatoes are very tender, then drain and let cool.

When the potatoes are cool enough to handle, peel away the skins and mash using a masher or potato ricer. Don't be tempted to mash the potatoes in a food processor—the texture becomes "gluey" rather than fluffy.

Add the garlic, 2 tablespoons of lemon juice, 1/2 teaspoon of salt, and white pepper to taste to the potatoes. Slowly beat in the oil, a tablespoon at a time, making sure each addition is well incorporated before you add more, until no more can be absorbed—the exact amount you will need will depend on the texture of the potatoes. Taste and add extra lemon juice and salt, as you wish. Set aside to cool completely, then transfer to a serving bowl, cover, and chill in the refrigerator for at least 2 hours.

Serve the sauce with a platter of the prepared vegetables and warmed pita bread, if desired.

Cook's tip
The sharp, pungent flavor of the raw garlic mellows after a day in the refrigerator, but if you still find the garlic taste too strong, stir in 1–2 tablespoons of strained plain yogurt.

Nut and bell pepper spread

Muhammara

Serves 4–6 as part of a mezze

2 large red bell peppers, rubbed with olive oil

about 1/3 cup olive oil, plus extra for covering (optional)

1 onion, chopped

1/2 tsp ground cumin

2 tbsp walnut pieces, toasted and chopped, plus extra to garnish

2 tbsp pine nuts, toasted, plus extra to garnish

2 tbsp cashews, toasted and chopped, plus extra to garnish

2 tbsp fresh white breadcrumbs

1/4 tsp dried chile flakes, or to taste

1/4–1/2 tsp pomegranate molasses

1–2 tbsp freshly squeezed lemon juice

salt

1/2 pomegranate, to garnish

Pita triangles, to serve (see right)

Most Middle Eastern recipes for this spread use walnuts only, but this is a lighter, sweeter version from Lebanon with the addition of pine nuts and cashews.

Preheat the oven to 450°F/230°C, or its highest setting, and line a small roasting pan with foil. Put the red bell peppers in the pan and roast in the preheated oven for 15–20 minutes, or until the skins are charred. Remove from the oven, cover with a folded clean kitchen towel, and let cool. When cool enough to handle, peel away the skins, then halve from top to bottom, seed, and thinly slice. Set aside.

Heat 3 tablespoons of the oil in a skillet. Add the onion and cook over medium heat, stirring, for 2 minutes. Add the cumin and cook, stirring, for an additional 2–3 minutes, or until the onion is soft.

Transfer the onion and any oil in the skillet to a food processor. Add the bell peppers, nuts, breadcrumbs, chile flakes, pomegranate molasses, 1 tablespoon of lemon juice, and salt to taste, and process until well mixed. With the motor running, drizzle in enough of the remaining oil to make a thick, spreadable paste. Taste and add extra lemon juice and/or salt, as you wish. Transfer to a serving bowl.

If not serving immediately, cover the surface with a thin layer of oil, then cover the bowl and refrigerate for up to 3 days. Stir in the oil before serving.

Just before serving, hold the pomegranate half over the surface, cut-side down, and tap the top with a wooden spoon so that the seeds fall out. Serve at room temperature with Pita triangles.

Pita triangles

These thin, crisp wedges of bread make an interesting alternative to ordinary pita bread. Preheat the oven to 350°F/180°C and split 4–6 pita breads in half to make 8–12 thin slices of bread in total, then cut each half into 4 wedges. Spread the wedges out, rough-sides up, on a cookie sheet. Lightly brush with olive oil and bake in the preheated oven for 20 minutes, or until crisp and light golden brown. Let cool slightly and serve warm or at room temperature with a selection of dips. Any leftovers can be stored in an airtight container for up to 3 days.

Falafel

Falafel

This popular choice for a mezze spread is served throughout the Middle East by street vendors, who deep-fry these "bean balls" to order and sell them wrapped in flat bread with lettuce, tomato, and cucumber and a good dollop of Sesame sauce.

Makes about 30

1/4 cup medium bulgur wheat

1 day-old pita bread, torn into small pieces

1 tbsp boiling water

1 onion, quartered

4 garlic cloves

2 tbsp coarsely chopped fresh flat-leaf parsley or cilantro

1 cup dried fava beans, rinsed and soaked in cold water for at least 12 hours

1 1/2 tbsp ground cumin

1 1/2 tbsp ground coriander

1 tsp ground turmeric

1 tsp baking powder

2 tsp salt

pepper

peanut or sunflower-seed oil, for deep-frying

To serve

lemon wedges (optional)

warmed Arab flat bread or pita bread

Sesame sauce, Chickpea dip, or Yogurt and cucumber dip, to serve

Put the bulgur wheat in a heatproof bowl and pour over enough boiling water to cover. Cover the bowl with a folded clean kitchen towel and let stand for at least 20 minutes. Put the pita bread in a separate bowl, sprinkle with the boiling water, and let soak in.

Put the onion and garlic in a food processor and process until finely chopped. Add the parsley and process again until finely chopped. Use your hands to squeeze the bread dry. Drain the beans, rinse, shake dry, and add to the food processor along with the bread. Process to a slightly grainy paste. Scrape the mixture into a large mixing bowl.

Use your hands to squeeze the bulgur wheat dry and add to the bowl with the cumin, coriander, turmeric, baking powder, the salt, and pepper to taste. Use your hands to mix all the ingredients together, then shape into about 30 equal-size balls, each about the size of a walnut, then flatten slightly to 1/2 inch/ 1 cm thick. Cover with plastic wrap and chill in the refrigerator for at least 30 minutes.

Heat enough oil for deep-frying in a deep-fat fryer or heavy-bottomed skillet to 350–375°F/180–190°C, or until a cube of bread browns in 30 seconds. Add the falafel, in batches to avoid overcrowding, and cook, turning once, for 6–8 minutes, or until brown. Remove with a slotted spoon and drain on a plate lined with crumpled paper towels while you cook the remaining falafel.

Serve warm or at room temperature with lemon wedges for squeezing over, if using, and accompanied by warmed flat bread or pita bread and Sesame sauce, Chickpea dip, or Yogurt and cucumber dip.

Spinach and feta pastry triangles

Spanakopita

Makes 12

12 sheets filo pastry, about
12 x 9 inches/30 x 23 cm each,
thawed if frozen

about 7/8 cup unsalted butter,
melted and cooled

Filling

9 oz/250 g baby spinach leaves,
any thick stems removed, rinsed,
and shaken dry

2 tbsp olive oil, plus extra for oiling

4 scallions, finely chopped

1 small garlic clove, crushed

2 tbsp chopped fresh dill

4 1/2 oz/125 g Greek feta cheese
(drained weight), crumbled

1 large egg, beaten

1/4 tsp freshly grated nutmeg

2 tbsp pine nuts, toasted (optional)

2 tbsp raisins (optional)

salt (optional) and pepper

Traditional Greek recipes don't include the raisins and pine nuts—they are an Arab touch that spread throughout the Mediterranean—but they are natural partners for the spinach and feta cheese.

To make the filling, put the spinach with only the water clinging to its leaves in a large pan, cover, and cook over medium heat, stirring occasionally, for 10 minutes, or until tender and reduced in volume. Tip into a colander or strainer resting in the sink and let cool. When cool enough to handle, use your hands to squeeze out all the excess moisture. Put in a large mixing bowl and set aside.

Heat the oil in the wiped-out skillet. Add the scallions and cook over medium heat, stirring frequently, for 1 minute. Add the garlic and cook, stirring, for an additional 1–2 minutes, or until the scallions are soft. Add to the bowl with the dill, feta cheese, egg, nutmeg, pine nuts, and raisins, if using, and pepper to taste—the texture will be very runny. Cook a small amount of the mixture in the skillet to see if it needs salt, but the salt in the feta cheese should be sufficient.

Preheat the oven to 375°F/190°C and lightly brush 1 or 2 cookie sheets with oil. Lay one sheet of filo pastry on a counter and brush all over with melted butter. Top with another sheet of filo and brush with butter, then add a third and again brush with butter. Cut the

3 layers into long strips 3 inches/7.5 cm wide. Cut a total of 12 sets of strips. Arrange one set of strips on the counter vertically in front of you. Keep the filo you are not using tightly covered with damp (not wet) paper towels so that it does not dry out.

Stir the filling and put 1 tablespoon in the bottom left-hand corner of the strip, about 1/4 inch/5 mm from the short edge. Gently lift the corner over the filling to form a triangle so that the bottom edge now runs along the right-hand side. Fold the triangle upward, then to the left so that the open edges are across the top and the filling is enclosed. Continue folding the triangle from side to side until you reach the top. Dab the small strip of pastry at the top with water and fold over the triangle to seal. Transfer to the prepared cookie sheet, seam-side down, and brush with melted butter. Repeat with the remaining sets of filo strips.

Bake in the preheated oven for 12–15 minutes, or until golden brown and crisp. Serve hot or at room temperature.

Cheese pastries

Sambusaks

Makes 22–24

Pie dough

scant 1 cup all-purpose flour, plus extra for dusting

5 1/2 heaping tbsp white vegetable fat, chilled and grated, plus extra for greasing

1/2 tbsp freshly squeezed lemon juice

about 5 tbsp water, chilled with an ice cube

1 egg yolk, beaten, to glaze

Filling

3 oz/85 g provolone cheese (drained weight), diced

scant 1/3 cup ricotta cheese (drained weight)

1 oz/25 g feta cheese (drained weight), crumbled

1 egg yolk

1 1/2 tbsp very finely chopped fresh mint or dill

finely grated rind of 1/2 lemon

salt (optional)

These pastries, with a mixed cheese and herb filling, are often deep-fried, but here they are baked for a lighter result. These are versatile in that they can be served hot or at room temperature, and can be assembled in advance for last-minute baking.

To make the pie dough, put the flour in a bowl and stir in the fat. Add the lemon juice and gradually add enough of the water, using a fork to bring the ingredients together, until a soft dough forms. Knead the dough into a rough ball on a very lightly floured counter, then wrap in plastic wrap and chill in the refrigerator for at least 30 minutes.

Meanwhile, to make the filling, put the provolone cheese in a food processor and process to fine crumbs. Add the ricotta and feta cheeses and egg yolk, and process again until well blended. Add the mint and lemon rind and process until just incorporated. Cook a small amount of the filling in a dry skillet to see if it needs salt, but the salt in the feta cheese should be sufficient. Scrape the filling into a small bowl, cover and chill in the refrigerator until required. (If you do not intend to serve the pastries immediately, the filling can be chilled for up to 24 hours.)

Preheat the oven to 400°F/200°C and lightly grease a cookie sheet. Divide the dough in half and roll out one half on a lightly floured counter with a lightly floured rolling pin until about 1/8 inch/3 mm thick. Using a floured 3-inch/7.5-cm round cutter, cut out 12 circles, rerolling the trimmings as necessary. Repeat with the remaining dough to make 22–24 circles in total.

Put 1 teaspoon of the filling on one half of a dough circle. Moisten all round the edge with water, then fold the dough over to form a half-moon shape and press the edges together. Dip the tines of a fork in flour, then press all round the edge to seal. Transfer the dough to the prepared cookie sheet. Repeat with the remaining dough circles. (At this point, the pastries can be covered with plastic wrap and refrigerated for several hours.)

Lightly brush the pastries with beaten egg yolk. Bake in the preheated oven for 15–18 minutes, or until golden brown. Serve warm or at room temperature.

Olives with lemon

Zayton was lemons

Serves 4–6 as part of a mezze

scant 1½ cups mixed large, plump green and black olives, rinsed if not in olive oil and patted dry

extra virgin olive oil

½ tsp ground coriander

1 tsp dried oregano or thyme

pinch of dried chili flakes (optional)

1 preserved lemon (see right), rinsed and thinly sliced

2 tsp chopped fresh dill or cilantro, to garnish

warmed pita bread or other Arab flat bread (optional), to serve

One of the simplest mezze you will ever come across is a bowl of green or black olives. In this recipe, the olives are flavored with spices, chili flakes, and preserved lemons for a distinctive Arab flavor.

Put the olives in a serving bowl and pour over enough oil to cover. Stir in the coriander, then add the oregano and chili flakes, if using. Stir in the preserved lemon slices.

Just before serving, sprinkle with the dill. Serve with warmed pita or other flat bread (optional) for mopping up the flavored oil. Alternatively, cover and refrigerate for up to 1 week. Any leftover olives will keep almost indefinitely in the refrigerator in an airtight container.

Cook's tip

When you put the olives in the refrigerator, the oil will become cloudy, but it will clear again as it returns to room temperature. Any leftover oil is delicious spooned over broiled provolone cheese or used in a salad dressing.

Preserved lemons

These flavor many dishes throughout the Arab world, especially Moroccan tagines. They are sold in Middle Eastern food stores and supermarkets, but are very easy to make, although you must allow several weeks for them to soak in the salty brine before using. Quarter 6 lemons, without cutting through the base, so that they open out like a flower. Rub the cut edges with coarse sea salt. Put 2 tablespoons of sea salt in the base of a large jar just big enough to hold the 6 lemons. Put 3 of the lemons in the jar, pressing them together, then cover with another thin layer of salt. Add the remaining lemons and sprinkle with another layer of salt. Squeeze over the juice from 2 more lemons. Cover the jar and refrigerate for at least 2 weeks, but ideally a month, turning the jar over once a day. The lemons will then be ready to be rinsed and used. They will keep for several months in the covered jar in the refrigerator.

Peppers with feta

Piperyiés yemistés me feta

Makes 12

4½ oz/125 g feta cheese (drained weight)

12 long, slender red or yellow peppers or short, thick fresh red chiles, rubbed with olive oil

extra virgin olive oil, for drizzling

pepper

arugula leaves, to garnish

For this simple recipe which can be prepared well in advance of serving, you need short, squat fresh red chiles, or the long, slender red or yellow peppers ("Romano" is one variety). If you can't find either variety, look for jars of peeled peppers.

Put the feta cheese in a bowl with warm water to cover. Let soak for 1 hour, changing the water 2–3 times.

Meanwhile, preheat the broiler to its highest setting. Put the peppers in a roasting pan and cook under the broiler, about 4 inches/10 cm from the heat, for 10 minutes, turning once, until the skins are just charred. Transfer to a bowl, cover with a folded clean kitchen towel, and let cool.

When cool enough to handle, peel away the skins, then cut off the tips so that they are about 1½ inches/4 cm long. Use a teaspoon to scrape out the seeds and membranes from the pepper tips, being careful not to tear the flesh.

Drain the feta cheese well, put in a bowl, and use a fork to mash into a thick paste. Put 1 teaspoon of the cheese in each pepper tip and use your fingers to push it into the cavity, handling gently to prevent tearing. Put on a serving plate, drizzle with oil, and season to taste with pepper. Cover and chill in the refrigerator until ready to serve. Just before serving, garnish with arugula.

Cook's tip

Seed the part of the peppers or chiles that you don't use in this recipe and use in the Red pepper salad, or thinly slice and stir into the Chickpea salad. Cut into bite-size pieces, they also taste good dipped into Sesame sauce.

Tunisian stuffed pastries with egg

Briks à l'oeuf

Makes 4

8 sheets filo pastry, about
12 x 7 inches/30 x 18 cm each,
thawed if frozen

about 4 tbsp unsalted butter,
melted and cooled

lemon wedges (optional), to serve

Filling

1½ tbsp olive oil, plus extra
for cooking

generous 1 cup lean fresh ground
lamb or beef

6 scallions, finely chopped

1 garlic clove, crushed

2 tsp ground cumin

2 tsp ground cinnamon

2 tsp ground ginger

½ tsp harissa paste, or to taste

2 tbsp chopped fresh flat-leaf
parsley, cilantro, or mint

about 4½ tbsp unsalted
butter, melted

4 small eggs, plus 1 beaten egg yolk

salt and pepper

In Tunisia, these deep-fried pastries are made with paper-thin semolina pie dough, called *malsouqua*, but commercial filo pastry makes an acceptable, convenient alternative. They are best served hot, but take care not to burn your tongue.

To make the filling, heat 1 tablespoon of the oil in a skillet. Add the meat and cook, stirring to break up any lumps, over medium heat, until no longer pink. Remove with a slotted spoon, leaving behind as much fat as possible. Add the remaining oil, then the scallions and garlic, and cook, stirring, for 1 minute. Add the spices and harissa paste and cook, stirring, for 2 minutes. Return the meat to the pan and stir in the parsley, and salt and pepper to taste. Remove from the heat and set aside.

Lay one sheet of filo pastry on a counter horizontally in front of you and brush with melted butter. Top with another sheet and brush with butter. Fold the left-hand edge over to the right-hand edge, as if closing a book, and brush with more butter. Fold in the edges, as necessary, to make a 6-inch/15-cm square. Keep the filo you are not using tightly covered with damp (not wet) paper towels so that it does not dry out.

Use a slotted spoon to put one-quarter of the filling in the upper left-hand corner, about ¾ inch/2 cm from the edges, and make a slight indentation in the center. Crack an egg into the indentation without breaking the yolk. Gently brush the edges with the beaten egg yolk, then lift the opposite corner over the filling to form a triangle. Press the edges together to seal, then brush the top with butter and set aside. Repeat with the remaining sheets of filo.

Heat a ½-inch/1-cm layer of oil in a large skillet over high heat, or until a cube of bread browns in 30 seconds. Add 1 or 2 pastries, depending on the size of your skillet, and cook for 1 minute, or until the underside is golden brown. Use a spatula to gently flip the pastries over and cook for an additional 45 seconds–1 minute until the other side is golden. Remove with a slotted spoon and drain on a plate lined with crumpled paper towels while you cook the remaining pastries, adding extra oil to the pan, if necessary. Serve immediately, with lemon wedges for squeezing over if desired.

Note

Because of the lightly cooked egg, this recipe should be avoided by infants, the elderly, pregnant women, convalescents, and anyone suffering from an illness.

Meat and Poultry

It is impossible to miss the inviting aroma of meat grilling when walking through the markets and restaurant districts throughout the region. But if a barbecue is impractical for you, use a ridged, cast-iron grill pan.

Marinades might once have been essential to mask the taste of inferior meat, but today they enhance the flavor. The milk-based marinade in the Shish kabobs recipe works well with beef as well as lamb.

Meatballs, always popular mezze, once involved hours of pounding meat with large pestles and mortars to tenderize it, but now food processors have eliminated the need for such laborious manual work.

Stuffed lamb and bulgur meatballs

Kibbeh mashi

These richly flavored meatballs, with a crisp meat and bulgur wheat casing around a spiced meat and pine nut filling, are often cited as one of the national dishes of Syria and Lebanon, where accomplished kibbeh makers are held in high esteem.

Makes 12

1¼ cups fine or medium bulgur wheat

1 cup fresh ground lamb

½ onion, chopped

½ tsp ground cumin

½ tsp ground allspice

½ tsp ground cinnamon

½ tsp salt

1–2 tbsp water (optional)

olive, sunflower-seed, or peanut oil, for deep-frying

lemon wedges or Yogurt and Cucumber Dip, to serve

Filling

1 tbsp pine nuts

1 tbsp olive oil

1 small onion, very finely chopped

scant ½ cup fresh ground lamb

½ tsp ground allspice

½ tsp pomegranate molasses (optional)

pinch of dried chili flakes, or to taste

1 tbsp finely chopped fresh flat-leaf parsley or cilantro

salt and pepper

Put the bulgur wheat in a heatproof bowl and pour over enough boiling water to cover. Cover the bowl with a folded clean kitchen towel and let stand for at least 20 minutes.

Meanwhile, to make the filling, heat a dry skillet, add the pine nuts, and cook, stirring over medium heat, just until golden brown. Immediately tip out of the skillet and set aside.

Heat the oil in the skillet, add the onion, and cook over medium heat, stirring, for 1 minute. Add the meat and cook, stirring to break up any lumps, until no longer pink. Return the pine nuts to the skillet and stir in the allspice, pomegranate molasses, if using, chili flakes, and salt and pepper to taste. Tip the filling into a bowl, stir in the parsley and let cool.

To make the outer casing, put the meat in a food processor and process to a thick paste. Drain the bulgur wheat and use your hands to squeeze dry. Add to the lamb paste along with the onion, spices, and salt and process again until well blended and pasty. With the motor running, slowly drizzle in some water, if necessary, to make a thick, smooth paste.

Knead the lamb paste back and forth several times on a counter. Using wet hands, roll the paste into 12 equal-size balls. Working with one ball at a time and wet hands, hold the ball in one hand and use the thumb and index finger of your other hand to make a hollow in the center. Add 1 tablespoon of the filling, then use your wet fingers to pinch the hole closed and seal the seam, shaping the mixture into a "teardrop." Repeat with the remaining balls, taking great care to smooth over the closing and any cracks, otherwise the casings will burst when fried.

Heat enough oil for deep-frying in a deep-fat fryer or heavy-bottomed skillet to 350–375°F/180–190°C, or until a cube of bread browns in 30 seconds. Add the kibbeh, in batches to avoid overcrowding, and cook for 3–4 minutes, turning frequently, until brown and crisp all over. Remove with a slotted spoon and drain on a plate lined with crumpled paper towels while you cook the remaining kibbeh. Serve hot with lemon wedges for squeezing over, or cooled with Yogurt and Cucumber Dip.

Deep-fried lamb meatballs

Kadin budu

Makes 16

1 cup lean fresh ground lamb

6 scallions, finely chopped

2½ tbsp long-grain rice

2 tbsp finely chopped fresh mint

½ tbsp salt, or to taste

2 eggs, beaten in a wide bowl

olive, sunflower-seed, or peanut oil,
for deep-frying

pepper

Yogurt and Cucumber Dip,
to serve (optional)

sprigs of flat-leaf parsley, to garnish

These delicious meatballs were once a delicacy prepared in Ottoman court kitchens. To ring the changes, replace the ground lamb with ground beef and replace the chopped mint with chopped fresh parsley or cilantro.

Put the ground meat in the food processor and process to a thick paste. Transfer to a bowl, add the scallions, rice, mint, salt, and pepper to taste (see Cook's tip) and use your hands to knead together. Wet your hands and roll the mixture into 16 equal-size, oval-shaped balls. At this point, the meatballs can be covered with plastic wrap and chilled in the refrigerator for several hours.

Put the meatballs in 1 or 2 skillets or sauté pans large enough to hold them in a single layer and pour over enough boiling water to cover by about 2 inches/5 cm. Return the water to a boil, then reduce the heat to low and let the meatballs simmer for 25 minutes, or until cooked through. The easiest way to check if they are cooked is to cut one open. Otherwise, insert a metal skewer—it should come out hot and the juices run clear. Remove with a slotted spoon and drain on a plate lined with crumpled paper towels, then pat dry.

Heat enough oil for deep-frying in a deep-fat fryer or heavy-bottomed pan to 350–375°F/180–190°C, or until a cube of bread browns in 30 seconds. Use 2 forks or a pair of tongs to dip the meatballs in the beaten eggs, making sure that they are coated all over. Let any excess egg drip back into the bowl, then add the meatballs to the oil, in batches to avoid overcrowding, and cook for 5–6 minutes, or until brown and crisp all over. Take care not to turn them too often in the hot fat, or they can fall apart. Instead, let one side cook, then gently roll them onto the other side. Remove with a slotted spoon and drain on a plate lined with crumpled paper towels. Keep hot in a low oven while you cook the remaining meatballs.

Serve the meatballs hot, garnished with flat-leaf parsley. Although Turks tend to serve these plain, the Yogurt and Cucumber Dip makes a delicious accompaniment.

Cook's tip

To check the amount of seasoning, fry a small amount of the raw lamb mixture in a dry skillet before shaping into meatballs. Remember that the rice will be bland tasting, so you might need more salt than you expect.

Shish kabobs

Şiş kebabı

Serves 4–6 as part of a mezze

1 lb 2 oz/500 g boneless leg or neck of lamb with a small amount of fat, cut into 3/4-inch/2-cm cubes

2 green bell peppers, halved, seeded, and cut into 3/4-inch/2-cm pieces

1 onion, quartered and separated into layers

2 cherry tomatoes per skewer

Marinade

2 tbsp milk

2 tbsp olive oil, plus extra for oiling

1 large onion, grated

1 tbsp tomato paste

1/2 tsp ground cumin

coarse sea salt and pepper

To serve

lemon wedges

warmed pita bread (optional)

Yogurt and Cucumber Dip

Food historians have long pondered the origins of the kabob. Although references to skewered meat cooked over fires appear in Persian texts predating the Ottoman Empire, scholars generally agree that the kabob as we know it developed in Turkey.

To make the marinade, put all the ingredients in a bowl and stir until the tomato paste is evenly dispersed. Add the lamb cubes and use your hands to coat well with the marinade. Cover and let marinate in the refrigerator for 2 hours. If you are using wooden skewers, soak them in cold water for at least 1 hour.

Heat a ridged, cast-iron grill pan over very high heat or preheat the broiler to its highest setting. Alternatively, light a barbecue and leave to burn until the flames die down and the coals are glowing. Lightly brush presoaked wooden or long, flat metal skewers with oil, then thread an equal quantity of the lamb cubes onto each one, occasionally interspersing with green bell pepper pieces, onion layers, and the cherry tomatoes. Sprinkle with sea salt.

Brush the grill pan or broiler rack with oil. Add the kabobs and cook, turning frequently and basting with the remaining marinade, for 8–10 minutes, or until the lamb and peppers are charred on the edges. Cut one lamb cube open to check that the meat is cooked to your liking.

Using a folded cloth to protect your fingers, hold the top of each skewer and use a fork to push the ingredients onto a serving platter. Serve immediately with lemon wedges for squeezing over, warmed pita bread, if using, and Yogurt and Cucumber Dip.

Beef and lamb koftas

Lahama mashvi koftas

Makes 12 koftas

scant 1 cup fresh ground beef

scant 1/2 cup fresh ground lamb

1/2 onion, grated

2 tbsp chopped fresh
flat-leaf parsley

1 tbsp chopped fresh cilantro

1 garlic clove, very finely chopped

1 tsp ground cumin

1/4 tsp ground cinnamon

1/2 tsp hot paprika, or to taste

1/2 tsp harissa paste, or to taste

1/2 tsp salt

pinch of cayenne pepper, or to taste

olive oil, for brushing

chopped fresh mint, to garnish

To serve

very finely shredded green cabbage

very thinly sliced red onions

chopped fresh flat-leaf parsley

extra virgin olive oil

lemon wedges (optional)

warmed pita bread

The wide variety of minced meat preparations throughout North Africa, the eastern Mediterranean, and the Middle East evolved out of a need to tenderize tougher cuts of meat. The harissa paste gives these meatballs a distinctly North African flavor.

Put the ground meat in a food processor and process to a paste. Add the onion, herbs, garlic, cumin, cinnamon, paprika, harissa paste, salt, and cayenne pepper and process again until blended.

Wet your hands and roll the mixture into 12 equal-size balls. Lightly brush 3–4 long metal skewers with olive oil. Press one meatball around one skewer and squeeze the 2 sides together to seal, then roll it back and forth in your palms to form an oblong "sausage" about 4 inches/10 cm long. Add 2 or 3 more meatballs to the skewer, depending on its length, and shape in the same way. Repeat with the remaining skewers. Cover with plastic wrap and chill in the refrigerator for at least 1 hour, but ideally up to 4 hours.

Heat a ridged, cast-iron grill pan over very high heat or preheat the broiler to its highest setting. Alternatively, light a barbecue and leave to burn until the flames die down and the coals are glowing. Brush the grill pan, broiler, or barbecue rack with oil. Add the meatballs and cook, turning once, for 8–10 minutes, or until slightly charred and springy to the touch. Cut one meatball open to check that the meat is cooked to your liking.

Meanwhile, toss the cabbage, onions, and parsley with a little extra virgin olive oil and salt and pepper to taste in a bowl, then spread out on a serving platter. Using a folded cloth to protect your fingers, hold the top of each skewer and use a fork to push the meatballs on top of the salad. Sprinkle with chopped mint to garnish. Serve with lemon wedges for squeezing over, if using, and warmed pita bread on the side.

Stuffed bell peppers

Biber dolmasi

Serves 6

olive oil, for cooking and baking

1 onion, finely chopped

1/2 tsp ground sumac

2 garlic cloves, finely chopped

generous 1 cup fresh ground lamb

1 tsp ground allspice

1/2 tsp ground cinnamon

large pinch of cayenne pepper, or to taste

5/8 cup basmati rice, rinsed, soaked in cold water for 30 minutes, and drained

2 tomatoes, grated, juices set aside, and skins discarded

2 tbsp blanched almonds, toasted and chopped

3 tbsp currants

2 tbsp chopped fresh flat-leaf parsley

2 tbsp chopped fresh mint

3 large green bell peppers

8 grape leaves preserved in brine, well rinsed and patted dry

1 tbsp tomato paste, dissolved in 1 1/4 cups boiling water

salt and pepper

This Turkish recipe is adaptable depending on the weather: the peppers can be served hot straight from the oven, lukewarm, or after being left to cool and chilled for several hours.

Preheat the oven to 350°F/180°C. Heat 3 tablespoons of oil in a skillet. Add the onion and sumac and cook over medium heat, stirring, for 3 minutes. Add the garlic and cook, stirring, for an additional 2 minutes, or until the onion is soft. Add the ground meat and cook, stirring to break up any lumps, until no longer pink. Stir in the allspice, cinnamon, cayenne pepper, and salt and pepper to taste and cook, stirring, for 1 minute.

Stir in the rice and tomatoes and their juices and bring to a boil. Continue boiling, stirring occasionally, for 3–5 minutes, or until the tomato juices have evaporated. Stir in the almonds, currants, and herbs and set aside.

Halve each green bell pepper from top to bottom, leaving the stalks intact, then seed. Divide the lamb mixture between the bell pepper halves.

Use the grape leaves to line the bottom of a shallow ovenproof casserole or deep skillet with an ovenproof lid and handle large enough to hold the pepper halves in a single layer. Arrange the pepper halves in the casserole or skillet so that they remain upright (see Cook's tip).

Spoon 1 tablespoon of the tomato paste liquid over each pepper half. Add 4 tablespoons of oil and salt and pepper to taste to the remaining tomato paste liquid, and pour around the bell peppers.

Bring the liquid in the casserole or skillet to a boil on the stove, then cover tightly. Bake in the preheated oven for 50 minutes–1 hour, or until the peppers are very tender and the rice is cooked. Taste and adjust the seasoning of the tomato liquid, if necessary, then serve the pepper halves hot, lukewarm, or chilled. If you let the peppers cool in the liquid in the covered container, they will absorb flavor from the grape leaves.

Cook's tip

If your casserole or skillet is too wide to hold the stuffed peppers upright, secure in place with uncooked potato wedges. The potatoes will be tender and have absorbed the flavors from the tomatoes and grape leaves when the peppers are cooked, so you can serve them alongside.

Albanian liver

Arnavut ciğeri

1 lb/450 g lamb's liver, rinsed and patted dry

1/2 tsp hot paprika, or to taste

4 tbsp all-purpose flour

sunflower-seed or peanut oil, for pan-frying

salt and pepper

To serve

1 red onion, thinly sliced

2 tbsp very finely chopped fresh flat-leaf parsley

1/2 tsp ground sumac (optional)

Despite the northern Balkan-sounding name, this is a popular Istanbul mezze, served at the restaurants that line the banks of the Bosporus. It is best served sizzling hot with the cool, raw onion salad.

First prepare the onion to serve with the liver. Put the onion slices in a bowl, sprinkle with the salt, and set aside to soften while you prepare the liver.

Use the tip of a small knife to lift up and peel away the thin membrane that covers the liver, then remove any tubes or gristle. Cut the liver into 1-inch/2.5-cm cubes. Sprinkle the liver cubes with salt to taste and use your hands to rub it in, then sprinkle the paprika over the cubes and again rub it in.

Put the flour and pepper to taste in a plastic bag. Add the liver cubes and shake until well coated. Tip into a strainer and shake to remove the excess flour. Transfer the liver to a plate and set aside. Wash the strainer to remove the flour and dry well.

Rinse the onion to remove the salt, then squeeze dry with your hands. Put in a serving bowl, toss with the parsley and sumac, if using, and set aside.

Heat a thin layer of oil in a large skillet over medium-high heat, until a cube of bread sizzles when dropped in the oil. Add the liver cubes, in batches if necessary to avoid overcrowding, and cook, shaking the skillet occasionally, for 2–2 1/2 minutes until brown on the outside but pink inside when you cut one open.

Hold the strainer over the sink and tip in the liver, shaking to remove any excess oil. Transfer the liver to the bowl with the onions and toss together. Serve immediately.

Sesame chicken wings

Fteroúyies kótas me sousámi

Economical and simple, this Greek-style mezze is good to serve when you are expecting a large number of guests with everyone arriving at different times, as the chicken wings are best served at room temperature.

Makes 24

4 tbsp olive oil, plus extra for oiling

finely grated rind and juice of 2 lemons

1 tbsp light brown sugar

pinch of cayenne pepper, or to taste

24 chicken wings, any small hairs removed and the thin tips cut off

2 tbsp sesame seeds

salt and pepper

Preheat the oven to 400°F/200°C and line a roasting pan with foil. Put a broiler rack in the pan.

Put the oil in a bowl, add the lemon rind and juice, sugar, cayenne pepper, and salt and pepper to taste and stir until the sugar has dissolved. Add the chicken wings and use your hands to coat well with the marinade. At this point, you can cook the wings immediately or cover and let marinate in the refrigerator for several hours.

Generously brush the broiler rack with oil. Arrange the wings on the rack in a single layer and sprinkle with the sesame seeds. If your broiler rack isn't large enough to hold all the wings, roast in batches. Roast in the preheated oven for 25–30 minutes until the chicken is tender and the juices run clear when a skewer is inserted into the thickest part of the meat, and the skin is crisp and the sesame seeds toasted. Transfer to a plate lined with crumpled paper towels and let cool before serving.

Vegetables and Salads

Vegetables form an important part of everyday meals throughout the Mediterranean, North Africa, and the Middle East, so vegetarians fare particularly well in the mezze culture. These are the recipes to turn to when temperatures are high, and light, simple food is most appealing.

Bread salad, originally a way of using up day-old bread, is a staple of Middle Eastern mezze tables. It offers lots of scope for creativity, as you can vary the ingredients with the best seasonal produce. This chapter also includes bean recipes that are a welcome addition to any mezze meal. The Chickpea salad is easy to pack and transport, so it also makes an ideal packed lunch or picnic dish, as does the Spinach omelet.

Egyptian brown beans

Fūl medames

Serves 4–6 as part of a mezze

1³/4 cups dried fava beans, rinsed and soaked in cold water for at least 12 hours with 1 tbsp baking soda

2 tbsp olive oil

1 onion, finely chopped

1 large garlic clove, crushed to a paste with 1 tsp salt

1 large tomato, seeded and finely chopped

salt and pepper

To serve

1 fresh red chile, seeded or not to taste and finely chopped, or ¹/2 tsp dried chili flakes (optional)

1 lemon, halved

extra virgin olive oil

warmed Arab flat bread or pita bread

Often called the national dish of Egypt, these earthy-flavored fava beans are eaten for breakfast or bought during the day stuffed in pita bread from street vendors—these are said to be a rich man's breakfast and a poor man's dinner.

Drain the beans and rinse well. Put in a pan with fresh cold water to cover and bring to a boil. Boil rapidly for 10 minutes, skimming off any foam that rises to the surface. Reduce the heat to low, cover, and simmer for at least 2 hours, or until tender enough to be easily mashed between your fingers, topping off the water as necessary. The exact simmering time will depend on how old the beans are—the older they are, the longer they will take. Drain the beans, reserving the cooking water. At this point, chefs and perfectionists insist that the beans should be peeled, but most home cooks don't bother—the choice is yours.

Heat the olive oil in a large skillet. Add the onion and cook over medium heat, stirring frequently, for 3 minutes. Add the crushed garlic and cook, stirring frequently, for an additional 2 minutes, or until the onion is very soft and golden but not brown. Use a slotted spoon to transfer half the beans to the skillet, stir, and mash into the onion. Add the remaining beans and tomato and heat through. Add salt and pepper to taste. If the mixture is too thick to be scooped up with flat bread, slowly add some of the reserved cooking water until you reach the desired consistency.

Spoon the beans into a serving bowl. Sprinkle the chile over the top, if using, then squeeze over juice from the lemon halves to taste and drizzle with extra virgin olive oil. Serve with warmed Arab flat bread or pita bread for scooping up the beans.

Chickpea salad

Salatat bi hummus

Serves 4–6

1/2 tbsp unsalted butter

1 tbsp olive oil

2 red onions, thinly sliced

about 3 tbsp extra virgin olive oil

about 1 tbsp freshly squeezed lemon juice

1/2 tbsp fresh thyme leaves or 1/2 tsp dried thyme

1/4 tsp ground cumin

1/4 tsp ground coriander

pinch of ground turmeric

14 oz/400 g canned chickpeas, drained, rinsed, and shaken dry

salt and pepper

To serve

2 tbsp chopped fresh dill, parsley, cilantro, or mint, plus extra to garnish

1 pomegranate, halved

With jeweled ruby pomegranate seeds, golden turmeric, and the vibrant green fresh herbs, this delicious salad evokes images of *One Thousand and One Arabian Nights*. Canned chickpeas are just as suitable and are more convenient than dried chickpeas.

Melt the butter with the oil in a heavy-bottomed skillet with a tight-fitting lid. Add the onions and cook over medium heat, stirring, until well coated in the butter and oil. Then reduce the heat to low, put a damp, crumpled piece of wax paper over the surface of the onions and cover the skillet. Let the onions "sweat" for 20 minutes, or until very soft and pale pink but not brown.

Meanwhile, mix 3 tablespoons of oil, 1 tablespoon of lemon juice, the thyme, spices, and salt and pepper to taste together in a bowl. Stir in the chickpeas.

Transfer the onions to a plate lined with crumpled paper towels and pat dry to remove the excess oil. Add to the chickpeas and stir together. Let cool, then cover and chill in the refrigerator for at least 1 hour.

Remove the chickpeas from the refrigerator 15 minutes before serving to return to room temperature. Taste and add extra lemon juice or oil, as you like, then stir in the chopped dill, parsley, cilantro, or mint. Hold the pomegranate over the salad, cut-side down, and tap the top with a wooden spoon until the seeds fall out. Repeat with the other half, then stir together, transfer to a serving bowl and serve. Garnish with the remaining herbs.

Tossed potatoes

Patates antinahtes

Serves 4–6 as part of a mezze

12–16 waxy, new potatoes, such as round red, scrubbed and patted dry
olive oil
1/2 cup full-bodied red wine
2 tbsp coriander seeds, crushed
salt and pepper
thyme leaves or chopped fresh flat-leaf parsley, to garnish

Cypriots tend to eat these straight from the skillet, but they are equally good served warm or at room temperature. You need a skillet with a tight-fitting lid large enough to hold the potatoes in a single layer, otherwise cook them in batches.

Put the potatoes in the largest skillet you have, or use 2 skillets, so that they are in a single layer. Pour over enough oil to cover the potatoes by 1/2 inch/1 cm and heat the oil over medium–high heat until shimmering with just a few bubbles breaking the surface but not boiling. Reduce the heat to very low, cover, and let the potatoes simmer for 10–12 minutes until they are very tender and the tip of a knife or a skewer slides in easily.

Drain the potatoes, then return to the skillet. Add the wine, crushed coriander seeds, and salt and pepper to taste, and bring to a boil over high heat. Continue to boil, uncovered, for 3–4 minutes, shaking the skillet occasionally to toss the potatoes around, until all the wine evaporates.

Tip the potatoes into a serving bowl and sprinkle with the thyme leaves to garnish. Serve hot or at room temperature.

Pan-fried cheese with red bell pepper salad

Saganáki me saláta piperyiés

In most Arab countries, Cypriot halloumi cheese is quickly pan-fried or grilled on a barbecue for this warm mezze, while Greeks prefer to use kasseri or kefalotyri cheese. If these cheeses are unavailable, use provolone instead.

Serves 4

8 slices halloumi, provolone, kasseri, or kefalotyri cheese, patted dry, if necessary, and cut into 1/2-inch/1-cm slices

about 2 tbsp all-purpose flour, for dusting

olive oil, for pan-frying

salt and pepper

lemon wedges, to serve (optional)

Red Bell Pepper Salad

2 large red bell peppers, rubbed with olive oil

scant 1/2 cup ripe, juicy black olives, rinsed if not in olive oil, pitted and sliced

4 scallions, finely chopped

about 3 tbsp extra virgin olive oil

about 2 tsp red wine vinegar

large handful of arugula leaves

To make the bell pepper salad, preheat the broiler to its highest setting. Put the bell peppers in a roasting pan and cook under the broiler, about 4 inches/10 cm from the heat, for 15 minutes, turning once, until the bell peppers collapse and the skins are charred. Transfer to a bowl, cover with a folded clean kitchen towel, and let cool.

When cool enough to handle, peel away the skins, then halve from top to bottom, seed and thinly slice the flesh. Put the bell pepper slices in a bowl with the olives, scallions, 2 tablespoons of extra virgin olive oil, and 2 teaspoons of vinegar and toss together. Add salt and pepper to taste and set aside.

Lightly dust each cheese slice with flour and shake off any excess. Heat a thin layer of olive oil in a large skillet, ideally nonstick. Add as many cheese slices as will fit in a single layer and cook over medium–high heat for 2 minutes, or until golden and crisp on the edges. Use a metal spatula to flip the cheese slices over and cook until golden on the other side. Transfer to a large platter. Cook the remaining cheese slices, adding more oil, if necessary.

Meanwhile, stir the arugula leaves into the pepper salad and sprinkle with salt and pepper to taste. Add a little more extra virgin olive oil or vinegar, as you like. Spoon the pepper salad alongside the fried cheese and serve immediately, with lemon wedges, if using, for squeezing over.

Spinach omelet

Eggah bi sabaneh

Serves 4–6 as part of a mezze

10½ oz/300 g baby spinach leaves, any thick stems removed, rinsed, and shaken dry

6 large eggs

6 scallions, finely chopped

4 tbsp chopped fresh herbs, such as chives, cilantro, dill, mint, and/or flat-leaf parsley, finely snipped or shredded

3½ oz/100 g canned chickpeas, drained, rinsed, and shaken dry

freshly grated nutmeg

3 tablespoons olive oil

1 tbsp butter

salt and pepper

Unlike fluffy French omelets, this Arab egg cake is in the style of Italian frittatas or Spanish tortillas—it is compact, solid, and easy to cut into wedges.

Put the spinach with only the water clinging to its leaves in a large pan, cover, and cook over medium heat, stirring occasionally, for 10 minutes, or until tender and reduced in volume. Tip into a colander or strainer resting in the sink and let cool. When cool enough to handle, use your hands to squeeze out all the excess moisture.

Beat the eggs in a large bowl, then add the spinach, scallions, herbs, chickpeas, nutmeg, and salt and pepper to taste and set aside. Preheat the broiler to high.

Heat a 10-inch/25-cm skillet with an ovenproof handle, ideally nonstick, over medium–high heat. Add the oil and swirl around so that the side and bottom are well covered. Add the butter and heat until sizzling, swirling the skillet.

Pour the egg mixture into the skillet and immediately use the back of a wooden spoon to smooth out, then reduce the heat to medium–low. Cook for 5 minutes, or until the base is golden brown, using a fork to draw the uncooked egg on the surface toward the center. When the base and side are set but the top is still runny, transfer the omelet to the broiler and cook, about 4 inches/10 cm from the heat, for 5 minutes, or until the top is set without any raw egg visible.

Invert the omelet onto a serving plate and use paper towels to mop up any oil on the surface. Set aside until just warm or at room temperature, then cut into wedges to serve.

Eggplants with yogurt

Patlican yoğurtla salatasi

Serves 4–6 as part of a mezze

1 large eggplant, about 1 lb 9 oz/ 700 g

1¼ cups strained plain yogurt

about 2 garlic cloves, crushed to a paste with ½ tsp coarse sea salt

olive oil, for cooking

salt

dried mint, to garnish

This is a classic example of the Arab love of combining hot and chilled ingredients. Eggplant slices absorb oil readily, so the oil must be at the correct temperature before you cook them. This seals the edges and prevents the slices becoming greasy.

Trim the ends of the eggplant, then cut into slices about ½ inch/1 cm thick. Fill a bowl large enough to hold all the eggplant slices with cold water, then add 2 tablespoons of salt and stir until dissolved. Add the eggplant slices and weight down with a plate so that they stay submerged, then let soak for 45 minutes.

Meanwhile, put the yogurt in a bowl and beat in the garlic. Taste and add extra garlic and/or salt, as you like, then cover and chill in the refrigerator.

Drain and rinse the eggplant slices, then pat dry. Heat a 2-inch/5-cm layer of oil in a large skillet to 350–375°F/180–190°C, or until a cube of bread browns in 30 seconds. Add as many

eggplant slices as will fit in a single layer and cook for 1 minute, or until dark golden brown. Use a metal spatula to turn the slices over and cook for 30 seconds–1 minute until browned on the other side. Transfer to a plate lined with crumpled paper towels and pat dry. Cook the remaining eggplant slices.

Arrange the hot eggplant slices on a plate and spoon the chilled yogurt sauce over. Sprinkle with dried mint to garnish and serve immediately.

Herb and cracked wheat salad

Tabbouleh

Serves 4–6

2/3 cup fine or medium bulgur wheat

3–4 tbsp freshly squeezed lemon juice

extra virgin olive oil, for covering

leaves from 1 large bunch of fresh flat-leaf parsley, shredded

leaves from 1 small bunch of fresh mint, shredded

6 scallions, finely chopped

2 tomatoes, peeled, seeded, and finely diced

salt and pepper

To serve

grape leaves preserved in brine, well rinsed and patted dry

romaine lettuce leaves, rinsed and shaken dry, or warmed Arab flat bread or pita bread (optional)

Lebanon and Syria both claim to be home to this bright green herb and wheat salad, but today it is popular around the world. In the West, wheat tends to be the dominant ingredient, while Middle Eastern salads put more emphasis on the herbs.

Put the bulgur wheat in a fine strainer and rinse under very hot running water. Use your hands to squeeze the bulgur wheat dry, then put in a large mixing bowl with 3 tablespoons of lemon juice. Pour over enough oil to cover, then set aside for at least 1 hour until the grains absorb the liquid and become tender.

Add the herbs, scallions, tomatoes, and salt and pepper to taste and toss all the ingredients together. Taste and add extra lemon juice, olive oil and/or salt and pepper, as you like. Serve immediately, or cover and chill in the refrigerator until required.

When ready to serve, line a bowl or platter with grape leaves and pile the salad on top. For an authentic Syrian touch, serve with lettuce leaves to scoop up the salad with, or serve with warmed Arab flat bread or pita bread alongside, if using.

Cook's tip
The longer the salad stands before serving, the more oil and lemon juice it will absorb, so taste before serving to see if it should be moistened. Be sure to give the salad a good stir before serving.

Mixed vegetable salad

Çoban salatasi

Every Middle Eastern country boasts their own version of this Turkish salad. What is common to all recipes, however, is the careful way in which the vegetables are cut into uniform dice. This is particularly good served alongside broiled meats.

Serves 4–6 as part of a mezze

1½ tbsp freshly squeezed lemon juice

1½ tbsp extra virgin olive oil

1 garlic clove, crushed to a paste with ¼ tsp salt

3 large, ripe tomatoes

2 red or green bell peppers

1 cucumber, about 7 oz/200 g

2 oz/55 g fresh flat-leaf parsley leaves, finely chopped

1 oz/30 g fresh mint leaves, finely chopped

salt and pepper

To serve

romaine lettuce leaves, rinsed and patted dry

warmed pita bread

Mix the lemon juice, oil, and garlic together in a large serving bowl and set aside.

Halve and seed the tomatoes, then cut the flesh into ¼-inch/5-mm cubes and add to the bowl. Halve and seed the bell peppers, then cut into ¼-inch/5-mm dice and add to the tomatoes. Halve the cucumber and use a teaspoon to scoop out the seeds, then cut into ¼-inch/5-mm dice and add to the other ingredients. Add the herbs and salt and pepper to taste.

Toss the salad together with your hands. Serve immediately with romaine lettuce leaves to scoop up mouthfuls of the salad, and warmed pita bread to mop up the juices.

Cook's tip
If you plan to make the salad in advance, sprinkle the cucumber dice with salt and let drain in a strainer resting in the sink for 20 minutes. Rinse well and pat dry before adding to the other ingredients.

Bread salad

Fattoush

Serves 4–6 as part of a mezze

1 cucumber

2 heads romaine lettuce, outer leaves removed and inner leaves torn into bite-size pieces

6 radishes, halved and cut into thin half-moon shapes

2 tomatoes, halved, seeded, and diced

4 scallions, finely chopped

1 green bell pepper, seeded and chopped

large handful of fresh flat-leaf parsley, finely chopped

1 tbsp dried mint

2 pita breads, split open

Dressing

6 tbsp fruity extra virgin olive oil

4 tbsp freshly squeezed lemon juice

pinch of ground sumac (optional)

salt

The Middle East's most ubiquitous salad. Although this originated as a way to use up day-old bread, all other ingredients should be fresh and in prime condition.

Halve the cucumber and use a teaspoon to scoop out the seeds. Chop each half into bite-size pieces. Put in a strainer resting in the sink, sprinkle with salt, and let drain for 20 minutes.

Meanwhile, preheat the broiler to high. To make the dressing, mix the oil, lemon juice, and salt to taste together in a serving bowl. Add the sumac, if using, then set aside.

Rinse the cucumber well to remove the salt, then pat dry. Add to the bowl with the dressing along with the torn lettuce leaves, radishes, tomatoes, scallions, green bell pepper, and herbs and toss together.

Toast the pita bread under the broiler on both sides until crisp and light brown. Tear the toast into bite-size pieces, add to the salad while still hot, and toss together. Serve immediately.

Cook's tip

The vegetables can be tossed in the salad dressing several hours in advance, covered and refrigerated, but it is best to add the bread just before serving.

Carrot salad

Salatat al jazar

Serves 4–6 as part of a mezze

1 lb 2 oz/500 g carrots, peeled but kept whole

2 tbsp olive or sunflower-seed oil

1 large garlic clove, finely chopped

1 1/2 tsp ground cumin

1 tsp salt

1 tsp sugar

1/2 tsp ground turmeric

1/4 tsp harissa paste, or to taste

about 4 tbsp freshly squeezed lemon juice

finely grated rind of 1 large lemon

2 tbsp chopped fresh flat-leaf parsley, to garnish

To serve

crumbled feta cheese

pitted black olives

This traditional Moroccan salad is interesting in that the carrots are first cooked and then grated and tossed with a spicy hot dressing before being chilled. The flavors are most refreshing when left to mingle overnight.

Bring a large pan of water to a rolling boil over high heat. Add the carrots, reduce the heat slightly, and cook for 10 minutes, or until tender. Drain well, reserving scant 1 cup of the cooking water, and let cool. When cool enough to handle, grate using a food processor fitted with a grater attachment or the coarse side of a box grater. Put in a heatproof bowl and set aside.

Heat the oil in a skillet, add the garlic, and cook over medium heat, stirring, for 1–2 minutes, or until soft but not colored. Stir in the cumin, salt, sugar, turmeric, and harissa paste and cook, stirring, for 30 seconds. Add 2 tablespoons of the lemon juice and all the rind along with 2/3 cup of the reserved cooking water, then bring to a boil, stirring. Reduce the heat and simmer for 5 minutes, then pour over the carrots and stir together so that the carrots are well coated with the dressing. Let cool completely. Cover and chill in the refrigerator overnight.

When you are ready to serve, stir the salad, add the remaining lemon juice to taste, and adjust the seasoning, if necessary. Sprinkle with the parsley to garnish, then stir in crumbled feta cheese and pitted black olives and serve.

Pickled turnips

Torshi lift

Makes about 500 g/1 lb 2 oz

1 lb 2 oz/500 g turnips, trimmed

1 small cooked beet, peeled and thinly sliced

1 fresh bay leaf

Pickling brine

1 1/4 cups water

2/3 cup white wine or cider vinegar

2 tbsp coarse sea salt

4 garlic cloves, sliced

1 tsp coriander seeds, crushed

1/2 tsp dried chile flakes (optional)

Throughout the Middle East, pickled vegetables are always served with other mezze dishes. Turnips are the traditional vegetable, but other pale vegetables, such as cabbage and cauliflower, can be given the same colorful treatment.

To make the brine, bring the water and vinegar to a boil in a nonreactive pan, then add the salt and stir until dissolved. Remove from the heat, stir in the garlic, crushed coriander seeds, and chile flakes, if using, and let infuse.

Meanwhile, bring a pan of salted water to a boil. Add the turnips and blanch for 5 minutes, then drain and let cool. When cool enough to handle, peel the turnips and cut them into 1/4-inch/5-mm slices. Layer the beet and turnips in a 3-cup jar.

Strain the cooled brine over the turnips, making sure that they are submerged—they must not be exposed to air. Tuck in the bay leaf, cover, and seal tightly, then set aside in a cool, dark place for 2 days, turning the jar over once a day. Transfer to the refrigerator for an additional 12 days before opening.

Variation

Pickled green chiles are another frequent feature of Middle Eastern mezze. Follow the recipe above, replacing the turnips with fresh green chiles and halving the quantity of these and all the other ingredients.

Beet salad

Saláta pantzári

Serves 4–6 as part of a mezze

2 lb/900 g raw beets

4 tbsp extra virgin olive oil

1$\frac{1}{2}$ tbsp red wine vinegar

2 garlic cloves, finely chopped

2 scallions, chopped

coarse sea salt

Garlic Sauce, to serve (optional)

While many Arab recipes for beet salad are served with thick, creamy yogurt alongside, Greeks favor a large dollop of Garlic sauce. It is also an excellent choice for a mixed mezze because it provides a refreshing contrast to broiled dishes.

Carefully remove the roots from the beets without cutting into the skin, then cut off all but 1 inch/2.5 cm of the stalks. Gently rub the beets under cold running water, without splitting the skins, to remove any dirt. Put the beets in a pan with water to cover and bring to a boil. Cover, reduce the heat slightly, and cook for 25–40 minutes, depending on the size, until the largest beet is tender when you pierce it with a long metal skewer or knife.

Meanwhile, put the oil, vinegar, garlic, scallions, and salt to taste in a jar with a screw-top lid and shake until emulsified, then set aside.

Drain the beets and rinse under cold running water until cool enough to handle, then peel away the skins. Thickly chop or slice the beets, then put in a bowl and pour over the dressing. Cover and chill in the refrigerator for at least 1 hour.

To serve, gently toss the salad and transfer to a serving platter. Serve with a bowl of Garlic Sauce on the side, if you like.

Fish and Seafood

Mezze cooks are blessed with abundant daily catches to choose from. Consequently, a selection of seafood recipes feature on most menus, especially at waterside cafés, tavernas, and restaurants. However, fresh fish and shellfish can be expensive away from ports, so think of these small-portion recipes as a chance to sample rarely enjoyed seafood.

The recipes in this chapter include Deep-fried squid rings, served hot with nothing more than lemon wedges for squeezing over, variations of which are served throughout the Mediterranean. Or for something more substantial try the Pan-fried fish with walnut and garlic sauce, a dish inspired by the Arab tradition of serving whole fish with creamy sauce.

Deep-fried squid rings

Kalamarákia tiganitá

Serves 4–6 as part of a mezze

olive oil, for deep-frying

about ³/₄ cup all-purpose flour

pinch of hot paprika or chili powder

1 lb 5 oz/600 g squid rings, and tentacles if available, rinsed and patted dry

salt and white pepper

sprigs of cilantro, to garnish

To serve

coarse sea salt

lemon wedges (optional)

Sesame sauce (optional)

Every Mediterranean country has its own twist on this dish, and this is one of the simplest recipes, with the squid lightly dusted with spiced flour before cooking. Deep-fry the rings at the correct temperature so that they don't become rubbery.

Heat enough oil for deep-frying in a deep-fat fryer or heavy-bottomed skillet to 350–375°F/180–190°C, or until a cube of bread browns in 30 seconds.

Meanwhile, put the flour, paprika, and salt and white pepper to taste in a plastic bag and shake together. Add the squid rings, and tentacles, if using, and shake until well coated. Use tongs to remove the squid pieces from the bag, shaking off any excess flour.

Add the squid pieces to the hot oil, in batches to avoid overcrowding, and cook, turning occasionally, for 3 minutes, or until golden brown. Remove with a slotted spoon and drain on a plate lined with crumpled paper towels. Sprinkle lightly with sea salt and keep hot in a low oven while you cook the remaining squid pieces. Make sure that the oil returns to the correct temperature between batches and remove any stray pieces of coating from the oil.

Serve hot, garnished with sprigs of cilantro, and with lemon wedges for squeezing over, if using. Sesame sauce also makes an excellent accompaniment.

Chile shrimp

Garides tiganités me tsíli

Serves 4–6 as part of a mezze

2 large garlic cloves, finely chopped

1 fresh red chile, chopped,
or 1 tsp dried chile flakes

5 tbsp olive oil

1 lb 5 oz/600 g large raw shrimp

salt

lemon wedges, to serve (optional)

This is one of the most popular mezze served in restaurants, tavernas, and bars all along the Mediterranean. Have lots of bread on hand to mop up the rich, spicy juices.

Put the garlic, chile, oil, and salt to taste in an ovenproof serving dish or individual ovenproof bowls. Break off and discard the shrimp heads, then peel away the shells. Devein the shrimp by using a small, sharp knife to make a shallow cut along the back, then use the tip of the knife to lift out the thin black vein. Add the shrimp to the oil and use your hands to rub the marinade all over. Cover and let marinate in the refrigerator for about 1 hour.

Preheat the oven to 450°F/230°C, or its highest setting. Stir the shrimp well, then bake in the preheated oven for 6 minutes, or until the shrimp turn pink, curl, and are cooked through when you cut into one. Serve straight from the oven in the dish or bowls with lemon wedges for squeezing over, if using.

Cook's tip
Fresh raw shrimp should always be cooked on the day they are bought, and refrigerated as soon as you get them home.

Batter-fried mussels

Midye tavasi

Serves 4–6 as part of a mezze

24–36 large live mussels
all-purpose flour, for coating
olive oil, for deep-frying

Batter

generous 1/3 cup all-purpose flour
1/4 tsp salt
1 tbsp olive oil
1 egg, separated
about 1/3 cup lager

To serve

coarse sea salt
lemon wedges
Sesame sauce or Walnut and garlic sauce (optional)

Served hot, straight from the fryer, these are a favorite mezze at the numerous tavernas along the Bosporus in Istanbul. The yeast in the lager makes a light batter that becomes crisp and golden when fried. Serve with one of two chilled sauces.

To make the batter, sift the flour and salt into a large mixing bowl and make a well in the center. Mix the oil and egg yolk together in a pitcher, then pour into the well. Gradually beat the liquid ingredients into the flour with a fork or whisk, gradually drawing in the flour from the side of the well. Slowly work in enough of the lager until a smooth coating batter forms. Cover and let stand at room temperature for at least 1 hour.

Meanwhile, clean the mussels by scrubbing or scraping the shells and pulling out any beards that are attached to them. Discard any with broken shells or any that refuse to close when tapped. Put them in a large, heavy-bottomed pan with just the water that clings to their shells, cover tightly, and cook over medium heat, shaking the pan frequently, for 3–4 minutes, or until the mussels have opened. Discard any mussels that remain closed. Drain and let cool, then remove from their shells. Cover and chill in the refrigerator until required.

Heat enough oil for deep-frying in a deep-fat fryer or heavy-bottomed skillet to 350–375°F/180–190°C, or until a cube of bread browns in 30 seconds. Meanwhile, stir the batter well. Beat the egg white in a separate bowl until stiff peaks form, then gently fold into the batter. Pat the mussels dry, then lightly coat with flour, shaking off any excess.

Add the mussels to the batter. Using 2 forks or a pair of tongs, transfer to the hot oil, in batches to avoid overcrowding, and cook for 1–2 minutes, turning once, until golden brown. Remove with a slotted spoon and drain on a plate lined with crumpled paper towels. Keep hot in a low oven while you cook the remaining mussels. Make sure that the oil returns to the correct temperature between batches and remove any stray pieces of batter from the oil.

Sprinkle the mussels with sea salt and serve immediately with lemon wedges for squeezing over, accompanied by a bowl of Sesame sauce or Walnut and garlic sauce, if using.

Swordfish kabobs

Kiliç şiş

Serves 4–6 as part of a mezze

1 lb 5 oz/600 g boneless swordfish steaks, about 1 inch/2.5 cm thick and cut into 1-inch/2.5-cm cubes
20 fresh bay leaves
olive oil, for oiling

Marinade

4 tbsp extra virgin olive oil
2 tbsp freshly squeezed lemon juice
1 garlic clove, crushed to a paste with 1/4 tsp salt
1/4 tsp white pepper
pinch of hot or smoked paprika, to taste
1 onion, halved and then cut into half-moon shapes
4 fresh bay leaves, torn in half

Dressing

5 tbsp extra virgin olive oil
5 tbsp freshly squeezed lemon juice
2 tbsp chopped fresh dill

Swordfish abounds off the coast of Turkey and this mezze is served at many of the harborside restaurants.

To make the marinade, whisk the oil, lemon juice, garlic, pepper, and paprika together in a nonreactive bowl. Add the swordfish cubes and use your hands to coat gently with the marinade. Sprinkle the onion and torn bay leaves over the top. Cover and let marinate in the refrigerator for at least 4 hours.

Meanwhile, make the dressing. Whisk all the ingredients together in a small bowl, cover, and set aside.

Put the whole bay leaves in a heatproof bowl, pour over enough boiling water to cover, and let soften for 1 hour. Drain well and pat dry. If you are using wooden skewers, let soak in cold water while soaking the bay leaves.

Heat a ridged, cast-iron grill pan over very high heat or preheat the broiler to its highest setting. Alternatively, light a barbecue and leave to burn until the flames die down and the coals are glowing. Lightly brush 4 long, flat metal skewers or presoaked wooden skewers with oil. Thread an equal quantity of the swordfish cubes and 5 bay leaves onto each skewer.

Lightly brush the grill pan, broiler, or barbecue rack with oil. Add the kabobs and cook, turning frequently and brushing with any of the remaining marinade, for 8–10 minutes until the swordfish feels firm.

Using a folded cloth to protect your fingers, hold the top of each skewer and use a fork to push the swordfish cubes and bay leaves onto a serving platter. Discard the bay leaves and serve immediately with the dressing for spooning over.

Tuna pastry rolls

Aton al boraq

Makes 8

12 sheets filo pastry, about
12 x 9 inches/30 x 23 cm each,
thawed if frozen

olive oil, for oiling and brushing

1 tbsp sesame seeds, to garnish

lemon wedges, to serve (optional)

Filling

7 oz/200 g canned tuna in oil,
drained and 1 tbsp of the oil
set aside

1 hard-cooked egg, shelled and
finely chopped

2 tbsp chopped fresh dill

1$\frac{1}{2}$ tbsp tomato paste

$\frac{1}{2}$ tsp harissa paste, or to taste

generous $\frac{1}{8}$ cup juicy, flavorsome
black olives, rinsed if not in olive oil,
pitted, and very finely chopped

salt and pepper

This is an easy version of a crisp filo pastry mezze made with canned tuna. It is best served hot, but it can also be left until cold and then packed for a picnic.

Preheat the oven to 375°F/190°C and lightly brush a cookie sheet with oil. To make the filling, put the drained tuna and the reserved oil, egg, dill, tomato paste, and harissa paste in a bowl and mash together until well blended. Stir in the olives and add salt and pepper to taste.

Lay one sheet of filo pastry on a counter and brush all over with oil. Top with another sheet of filo and brush with oil, then add a third and again brush with oil. Cut the 3 layers into long strips 4$\frac{1}{2}$ inches/12 cm wide. Cut a total of 8 sets of strips. Arrange one set of strips on the counter vertically in front of you. Keep the filo you are not using tightly covered with damp (not wet) paper towels so that it does not dry out.

Spoon one-eighth of the filling across the top center of the pastry in a line about $\frac{1}{2}$ inch/ 1 cm from the top edge and $\frac{1}{2}$ inch/1 cm from each side. Fold the top edge of the pastry over the filling and make one tight roll toward you. Fold in both long sides down the length of the filo so that the edges face the center. Continue rolling the filo over the filling until you reach the bottom. Transfer to the prepared cookie sheet, seam-side down. Repeat with the remaining sets of filo strips.

Brush the pastries with oil and lightly sprinkle with the sesame seeds. Bake in the preheated oven for 12–15 minutes, or until crisp and golden brown. Transfer to a plate lined with crumpled paper towels and let cool slightly before serving with lemon wedges, if using.

Pan-fried fish with walnut and garlic sauce

Samak maglu

Cold baked whole fish bathed in this creamy sauce (*tarator*) is a traditional Middle Eastern favorite for large gatherings, but here, tender fish fillets, for smaller mezze-size portions, are served hot with the chilled sauce.

Serves 4 as part of a mezze

4 white fish fillets, such as bass, bream, or red snapper, about 4¹⁄₂ oz/125 g each

1–2 tbsp olive oil, for pan-frying

lemon wedges, to serve (optional)

Marinade

¹⁄₂ cup fruity olive oil

2 fresh bay leaves, torn in half

1 garlic clove, finely chopped

2 tbsp chopped or snipped fresh herbs, such as flat-leaf parsley, rosemary, thyme, marjoram, or chives

salt and pepper

Walnut and garlic sauce

2 slices day-old bread, about 2 oz/55 g, crusts removed, and torn into small pieces

2 tbsp milk

1 cup walnut halves

3 garlic cloves

about 2 tbsp freshly squeezed lemon juice (optional) or white wine vinegar

about 1 cup olive oil

To make the marinade, mix all the ingredients together in a flat ovenproof dish. Add the fish fillets and gently turn in the marinade to coat. Cover and let marinate in the refrigerator for 2–4 hours.

Meanwhile, to make the sauce, sprinkle the bread with the milk. Put the walnuts and garlic in a food processor and process until very finely chopped. Add the bread, 2 tablespoons of lemon juice, and 3 tablespoons of the oil and process again to a thick, sticky paste. With the motor running, drizzle in enough of the remaining oil until the sauce is smooth and a pouring consistency. Add salt to taste, then add extra lemon juice, if you like. Transfer to a bowl, cover, and chill in the refrigerator while the fish is marinating.

Heat a large skillet, ideally nonstick, over high heat until a splash of water "dances" on the surface. Heat 1 tablespoon of oil, add as many fish fillets as will fit in a single layer, flesh-side down, and cook for 5 minutes, or until golden brown. Use a spatula to turn the fillets over and cook for an additional 1–2 minutes, or until the flesh feels firm and is opaque when you cut into one fillet. Transfer to a plate lined with crumpled paper towels. If all the fillets won't fit in your skillet in a single layer, keep hot in a low oven while you cook the remaining fillets, adding another tablespoon of oil to the skillet, if necessary.

Spread a thin layer of the sauce on a serving plate, then top with the fish fillets, flesh-side up. Serve immediately with lemon wedges for squeezing over, if using.

Broiled sardines with chermoula

Chermula sardines

Serves 4 as part of a mezze

12 sardines, heads removed,
cleaned, and rinsed

olive oil, for rubbing and oiling

coarse sea salt, for sprinkling

coarsely torn cilantro, to garnish

lemon wedges, to serve

Chermoula

1½ oz/40 g fresh cilantro leaves

1 oz/25 g fresh flat-leaf
parsley leaves

1½ tbsp ground cumin

1 tsp smoked paprika

½ tsp cayenne pepper, or to taste

3 tbsp freshly squeezed lemon juice

1 tsp salt

about 3 tbsp olive oil

Moroccan food is known for its highly spiced, bold flavors. This recipe features *chermoula*, a spicy garlic and herb sauce that packs quite a punch. It is one of the classics of Moroccan kitchens, used with meat and fish dishes alike.

To make the chermoula, put the herbs, spices, lemon juice, and salt in a food processor and process until finely chopped and blended. Add 3 tablespoons of oil and process again to a thick sauce, adding extra oil, if necessary.

Spread 1 teaspoon of the chermoula on the inside of each sardine. Cover and let marinate at room temperature for 15 minutes, or cover and let marinate in the refrigerator for 2–4 hours.

Heat a ridged, cast-iron grill pan over very high heat until a splash of water "dances" on the surface or preheat the broiler to its highest setting. Alternatively, light a barbecue and leave to burn until the flames die down and the coals are glowing. Rub the sardines with oil and lightly sprinkle with sea salt.

Brush the grill pan, broiler, or barbecue rack with oil, add the sardines, and cook for 3 minutes. Use a spatula to turn the sardines over, sprinkle with more salt, and cook for an additional 2 minutes, or until slightly charred and cooked through. Be prepared for some sardine skin to stick to the grill pan, broiler, or grill rack. Serve immediately garnished with cilantro and with lemon wedges for squeezing over.

Index